Show Me the Pretty Bird!

A Comedy in Two Acts about Being a
Bird Person in a World That Isn't

by Laurel A. Rockefeller

Show Me the Pretty Bird

This play is based on actual events in the life of author Laurel A. Rockefeller.

Table of Contents

Prologue

LAUREL stands downstage on the apron and addresses the audience.

LAUREL

(Singing to the tune of "the Brady Bunch" theme)

HERE'S A STORY OF A LOVELY LADY. WHO WAS BRINGING UP TWO VERY LOVELY BIRDS. BOTH OF THEM WITH SNOWY CRESTS, LIKE THEIR MOTHERS. THE YOUNGEST ONE WITH PEARLS.

(Switching to normal voice)

If you are like most people, you have never heard lyrics quite like that applied to that song! In fact, if you are like most people, you have no clue what the _______ I just said. How do birds have pearls?

Now of course if you are a *cockatiel* person, you are thinking, 'yeah, of course one has pearls – but most pearl cockatiels don't have white crests. Is this cockatiel a whiteface pearl?'

If you are *really* a cockatiel person you immediately want to know the exact genetic history of my bird – Arwen in this case. To which I am happy to tell you that Arwen is a dominate silver whiteface pearl pied hen and granddaughter of a National Cockatiel Society champion named Caspian. Her mother, Caspian's daughter, was Cloud, a whiteface pearl pied hen. Arwen's father was named Sterling and he was a dominate silver whiteface pearl pied.

Are the rest of you completely lost yet? Yeah, I thought so! That's because you are used to dog and cat breeds where people value uniform traits. When I say 'Cavalier King Charles Spaniel' you know exactly what that dog looks like. Mix another breed with that beautiful cav and you end up with a cute, lovable mutt who will never win the Westminster Kennel Club Dog Show.

But parrots are literally of a different class – Aves – and order – Psittaciformes – from we mammals. All captive raised parrots are wild animals socialized around humans, but still retaining their wild instincts. Selective breeding has created what we call 'colour mutations' that only change the plumage of our captive raised birds, usually by suppressing a specific hue like yellow – for pied cockatiels – or grey – for lutino cockatiels.

Show Me the Pretty Bird

With cockatiels, the more of these mutations a bird has, the better – in most cases. Therefore, a whiteface lutino cockatiel – which is what my older bird Mithril is – is more prized than a regular lutino cockatiel. Combining whiteface and lutino gives you a very different looking bird. In this case, a whiteface lutino which has all white feathers, pink eyes, pink beak, pink skin, and pink nails.

Are you ready for the science lecture to be over yet? Okay! Good! I swear the point of getting together today is *not* actually to trick you into a zoology class! Rather we are gathered today to celebrate the wonders that come with living with cockatiels – and the crazy things I encounter in my regular life when I'm around people who aren't as in love with these amazing and incredibly bright balls of feathered mischief.

On a technical note I want to mention that what you are about to watch is not always presented in chronological order. All of my cockatiels across the years have something to say – or do – that conveys the magic that is life with cockatiels.

Part tornado, part fluffy ball of feathers, and mixed with insane capacities for mischief, life is never dull around cockatiels. By the end of this show, you will know *exactly* what I mean.

(END OF SCENE)

Act I: Me and My Bird

Act I, Scene I

2010. Ocean Ave. apartment, Brooklyn New York. MITHRIL
sits under a small dining table surrounded by chairs. LAUREL
ENTERS and starts frantically looking for her.

LAUREL

Mithril? Mithril. Mithril!!!

(the search becomes more frantic as she fails to find Mithril)

Mithril! Where are you? Oh please, birdy! Where are
you! Don't die on me! Please! Please! Please be okay!

At length, Laurel looks under the dining table and locates
Mithril. Crawling down on the floor, she picks up Mithril and
holds her close.

LAUREL

Oh thank God I found you! Why did you do that?
Why didn't you tell me where you were?

Mithril stays silent. After giving Mithril some kisses, Laurel
puts her back on the top of her cage.

Laurel A. Rockefeller

9

(END OF SCENE)

(END OF SCENE)

Show Me the Pretty Bird

Act I, Scene II

LAUREL stands on the stage apron, the rest of the stage curtained off. She speaks directly to the audience, walking about casually, telling a story.

LAUREL

Many years ago, back when Mithril was just a baby, I was involved in a number of online bird clubs – in addition to the one in New York City that I became spokesperson for. I met a lot of great people there and it was at these meetings, often held at Starbucks or its competitors, that I first learned that I know more about cockatiels than the typical person.

Popular at the time was a story I usually called "A Parrot Thanksgiving," but its real name was "How to Stuff Your Turkey on Thanksgiving." Here's how it goes: "Get up early in the morning & have a cup of coffee. It's going to be a long day, so place your Parrot on a perch nearby to keep you company while you prepare the meal.

Remove Parrot from kitchen counter and return him to perch. Prepare stuffing, and remove Parrot from edge of stuffing bowl and return him to perch. Stuff turkey & place it in the roasting pan, and remove Parrot from edge of pan and return him to perch.

Have another cup of coffee to steady your nerves.

Remove Parrot's head from turkey cavity and return him to perch, and re-stuff the turkey. Prepare relish tray, and remember to make twice as much so that you'll have a regular size serving after the Parrot has eaten his fill.

Remove Parrot from kitchen counter and return him to perch.

Prepare cranberry sauce; discard berries accidentally flung to the floor by Parrot.

Peel potatoes, remove Parrot from edge of potato bowl and return him to perch.

Arrange sweet potatoes in a pan & cover with brown sugar & mini marshmallows.

Remove Parrot from edge of pan and return him to perch. Replace missing marshmallows.

Brew another pot of coffee. While it is brewing, clean up the torn filter. Pry coffee bean from Parrot beak. Have another cup of coffee & remove Parrot from kitchen counter and return him to perch.

When time to serve the meal: Place roasted turkey on a large platter, and cover beak marks with strategically placed sprigs of parsley.

Put mashed potatoes into serving bowl; rewhip at last minute to conceal beak marks and claw prints. Place pan of sweet potatoes on sideboard; forget presentation as there's no way to hide the areas of missing marshmallows.

Show Me the Pretty Bird

Put rolls in decorative basket, remove Parrot from side of basket and return him to perch. Also remove beaked rolls, serve what's left.

Set a stick of butter out on the counter to soften – think better and return it to the refrigerator.

Wipe down counter to remove mashed potato claw tracks.

Remove Parrot from kitchen counter and return him to perch.

Cut the pie into serving slices. Wipe whipped cream off Parrot's beak and place large dollops of remaining whipped cream on pie slices.

Whole slices are then served to guests, beaked-out portions should be reserved for host & hostess.

Place Parrot inside cage & lock the door. Sit down to a nice relaxing dinner with your family accompanied by plaintive cries of "want dinner!" from the other room."

Now what makes this story so funny is: it's absolutely true! Even if the details are different for your Thanksgiving holiday and you have a different flock configuration from the generic parrot in the popular story, I swear to God! Something like this happens every year when you have a parrot – and usually when you have any kind of bird with the freedom to join you out of cage and into your home too. So beware: finches and doves love to do all of this too!

Remember: there is never a dull moment around parrots!

(END OF SCENE)

Act I, Scene III

2010. Ocean Ave. apartment, Brooklyn New York. LAUREL sits at her laptop computer located on the dining table. MITHRIL relaxes in her cage. We hear the sound of wings in flight. ARAGORN sits on top of the refrigerator for a bit before falling down to the floor in the small space between the wall and the refrigerator.

LAUREL

(noticing the sound of wings)

Mithril? Aragorn?

(finds Mithril in cage)

Oh, there you are, Mithril! Where's Aragorn?

Mithril chirps pleasantly before switching to screams and contact calls.

LAUREL

Aragorn? Aragorn. Aragorn!

Aragorn chirps. Laurel locates him.

LAUREL

Aragorn? How did you get there? Birdy! I don't know how to get you out! I can't move the refrigerator! Oh Aragorn! What do I do?

(pacing)

Aragorn, I really don't know how to get you out from there! Oh my God! What do I do?

Laurel puts hand along top of fridge until able to bring hand down to where he is. Aragorn hops onto her hand which she slowly brings up and out.

LAUREL

Why did you do that, Aragorn? You scared me!

(Aragorn chirps)

Goofy ball of feathers! Little Sméagol! Yes! You are! You're such a Sméagol!

Laurel carries Aragorn back to the cage. Both birds chirp happily.

Show Me the Pretty Bird

(END OF SCENE)

Act I, Scene IV

2023, July. Vine Street Tower apartment, Johnstown, Pennsylvania. LAUREL sits at her desktop computer, working. ARWEN flies over and sits on the corner of the desk.

LAUREL

Hi Arwen! Watcha doin'?

(looks at Arwen's feet)

Arwen?

(notices one toe looks severely swollen)

Arwen? Oh my god! Arwen! Your toe! It's infected! How did that happen?

(turns back to the computer and frantically searches through google and several websites)

Oh my god! Oh my god! Oh my god! You need a vet! This sounds absolutely horrible! Oh please, birdy! Don't be sick! Please be okay.

(Arwen preens her feet. The "infected" material falls off harmlessly.)

What the – what? This isn't an infection at all! It's poop! You stepped into poop and it dried on your toe so it looks like an infection! Oh Arwen! Pretty Arwen! I love you Arwen!

(END OF SCENE)

Act I, Scene V

2024. January 5. Vine Street Tower apartment, Johnstown, Pennsylvania. Laurel sits at her desk. Arwen flies over and immediately attacks the mouse, mouse pad, and papers.

LAUREL

Arwen? Watcha doin'? No! No! Arwen! Stop! No, you cannot have my mouse. I need my mouse. Stop it!

(wrestling the mouse from Arwen's beak)

Arwen, no! Because I cannot work without the mouse, that's why! Stop it!

(shoos Arwen across the desk)

Come on, birdy! Let mommy work! Yes, I mean it!

(Arwen flies to nearby cage and pouts. Laurel gets up and tries to sooth ruffled feathers)

Don't hate me, birdy! Oh Arwen! I love you, birdy! Really!

Show Me the Pretty Bird

(LIGHTS FADE OUT)

(END OF SCENE)

Act I, Scene VI

2010. Ocean Ave. apartment, Brooklyn New York. MITHRIL and ARAGORN are hanging out on top of their floor cage. LAUREL ENTERS and addresses the audience.

LAUREL

I love to sing. When you have a good voice, cockatiels notice and like to join in with their unique and often very individual versions of singing, whistling, and talking. As I got to know Mithril and Aragorn, I discovered that there were three songs in particular that would get a vocal reaction from them, each of them with high notes they found irresistible: "Sing" by Joe Raposo, "It's a Small World" by Richard M. Sherman and Robert B. Sherman, and the title song "The Phantom of the Opera" by Andrew Lloyd Weber.

The year is 2010 and it's time for a cockatiel sing-along. If you know the songs, please join in! Let's see if we can get both Mithril and Aragorn to make some music!

Laurel approaches the cage and begins to sing "It's a Small World."

LAUREL

IT'S A WORLD OF LAUGHTER, A WORLD OF
TEARS. IT'S A WORLD OF HOPES AND A
WORLD OF FEARS. THERE'S SO MUCH THAT
WE SHARE THAT IT'S TIME WE'RE AWARE
IT'S A SMALL WORLD AFTER ALL.

IT'S A SMALL WORLD AFTER ALL. IT'S A
SMALL WORLD AFTER ALL. IT'S A SMALL
WORLD AFTER ALL. IT'S A SMALL, SMALL
WORLD.

Aragorn starts to whistle tentatively each time the high note
on "small" is sung, but stopping his whistle in the middle of
"world."

LAUREL

(to audience)

I swear, he normally sings along to this tune. Maybe
you can help me get him to sing?

THERE IS JUST ONE MOON AND ONE
GOLDEN SUN. AND A SMILE MEANS
FRIENDSHIP TO EV'RYONE. THOUGH THE
MOUNTAINS DIVIDE AND THE OCEANS ARE
WIDE IT'S A SMALL WORLD AFTER ALL.

IT'S A SMALL WORLD AFTER ALL. IT'S A
SMALL WORLD AFTER ALL. IT'S A SMALL
WORLD AFTER ALL. IT'S A SMALL, SMALL
WORLD.

(to audience)

Clearly Aragorn only likes the high notes today. Let's
see if he likes "Sing" today.

(changing tune to "Sing" by Joe Raposo and singing to Mithril
and Aragorn)

SING, SING A SONG.

(Aragorn starts to whistle tentatively)

SING OUT LOUD. SING OUT STRONG.

(Aragorn sings out a melody or harmony of his own design)

SING OF GOOD THINGS NOT BAD. SING OF
HAPPY, NOT SAD. SING, SING A SONG. MAKE
IT SIMPLE TO LAST YOUR WHOLE LIFE
LONG. DON'T WORRY THAT IT'S NOT GOOD
ENOUGH FOR ANYONE ELSE TO HEAR. JUST
SING, SING A SONG.

(to audience)

Come on! Join me!

LA LA LA LA LA LA LA LA LA LA LA LA LA LA
LALA LA LA. LA LA LA LA LA LA LA LA LA LA
LA LA LA LA LA LA LA LA.

MITHRIL

(sing/speaking)

Pretty bird! Pretty bird! MITHRIL! MITHRIL!

LAUREL

(to Mithril)

Mithril is a pretty bird! Yeah, you're a pretty bird!
Come on! Sing with us!

(to all)

SING, SING A SONG. LET THE WORLD SING
ALONG. SING OF LOVE THERE COULD BE.
SING FOR YOU AND FOR ME. SING, SING A
SONG. MAKE IT SIMPLE TO LAST YOUR
WHOLE LIFE LONG. DON'T WORRY THAT
IT'S NOT GOOD ENOUGH FOR ANYONE
ELSE TO HEAR. JUST SING, SING A SONG!

LA LA LA LA LA LA LA LA LA LA LA LA LA LA
LALA LA LA. LA LA LA LA LA LA LA LA LA LA
LA LA LA LA LALA LA LA.

Laurel A. Rockefeller

A round of sort forms as Laurel, the audience, Mithril, and Aragorn repeat the first verse and chorus with Ad Lib bird whistles, songs, and speech. Continue singing either or both verses for as long as desired by Director and as audience participation merits.

LAUREL/AUDIENCE

SING, SING A SONG. SING OUT LOUD. SING OUT STRONG. SING OF GOOD THINGS NOT BAD. SING OF HAPPY, NOT SAD. SING, SING A SONG. MAKE IT SIMPLE TO LAST YOUR WHOLE LIFE LONG. DON'T WORRY THAT IT'S NOT GOOD ENOUGH FOR ANYONE ELSE TO HEAR. JUST SING, SING A SONG.

LA LA LA LA LA LA LA LA LA LA LA LA LA LA LALA LA LA. LA LA LA LA LA LA LA LA LA LA LA LA LA LA LALA LA LA.

LAUREL

(finishing the song)

JUST SING, SING A SONG!

Show Me the Pretty Bird

(END OF SCENE)

(END OF ACT I)

Act II: Facing A World that Doesn't Love Birds

Show Me the Pretty Bird

Act II, Scene I

LAUREL stands on the stage apron in front of the curtain.

LAUREL

Well that was fun. I love to sing, don't you? Singing with my cockatiels is one of the great joys in life. Whether it's formal music written by others or just something I invent in the moment, it's always fun to be vocal with a bird. Sadly, not everyone thinks so too.

When Mithril was about a year and a half old I moved to Brooklyn New York with Mithril and Aragorn. My roommate in that first apartment I call "Kurt" in my biography "Mithril and Me: a Love Story." Kurt adored Mithril back when I lived in New Jersey. But sharing a home together was a different story altogether.

LAUREL EXITS. CURTAIN OPENS to reveal East 19th Street apartment living room. KURT sits at his computer. We hear flap of wings. LAUREL ENTERS running after Mithril and catches her.

KURT

I told you to keep your birds in their room!

LAUREL

What's wrong with Mithril flying out here? She's not hurting anything.

KURT

I don't want her here. That's enough. What if she destroys my stuff? She chews wood! Are you going to replace the frame on my painting if she does?

LAUREL

Kurt, she's not doing anything. Look! She's just sitting on my hand. She's a good bird.

KURT

Yeah, until she flies over to my painting and wrecks it.

LAUREL

She's not going to wreck it.

KURT

Yes she is! She's going to poop all over it.

LAUREL

No, she's not! Even if she sits there for a couple minutes, she's not wrecking anything!

KURT

Get your bird out of my house!

LAUREL

My apartment too! I'm on all the paperwork, same as yours.

KURT

I make more money than you do.

LAUREL

So? I pay equal rent as you do.

KURT

Get that bird out of my house!

LAUREL

No! She's a good bird and besides, you loved her when we didn't have an apartment together.

KURT

She's just a bird, what's the big deal?

LAUREL

Just a bird? Just a bird?

KURT

You don't need a bird. You have me.

Careful to not drop Mithril, Laurel backs off and steps away from Kurt.

Show Me the Pretty Bird

LAUREL

(struggling to control her anger)

I have you. I have you. And I shouldn't have Mithril?
I shouldn't have Mithril – but I have you? Wow! Oh
my God I really don't know what to say to that!

(to audience)

What do you think I should do, folks? Should I dump
this guy?

(to Kurt)

I'm going to pretend I didn't hear that, Kurt. I'm going to
pretend that you are the same guy I agreed to get an apartment
with back when we lived in New Jersey, back when you and
Mithril were best friends.

Laurel walks down to center downstage, still keeping Mithril in
her hands. LIGHTS FADE OUT over KURT who EXITS.
Lights focus on Laurel as she addresses the audience.

Laurel A. Rockefeller

LAUREL

(to audience)

It took years before I could get Kurt out of my life. But we
eventually escaped and only saw Kurt briefly when he bird sat
for me so I could travel to Chicago to teach a couple classes at
Royal University Midrealms in November, 2010. Naturally
even living with my birds for four years meant he couldn't
care for them properly, completely messing up their water
supply while I was gone for three days. After I retrieved my
apartment keys I never saw Kurt again. Mithril couldn't be
happier. Good riddance!

(END OF SCENE)

Act II, Scene II

2009. Brooklyn, New York. A shelter adjacent to a large field where horses are practicing agility. Mithril is sitting in her travel cage on a table. LAUREL arranges research papers, small wood/grapevine/leather bird toys, and plates of parrot foods nearby. To Laurel's left and right SCADIANS also set up their displays of medieval arts and crafts and works on projects. One sits and spins with a drop spindle. MOTHER and CHILD ENTER STAGE RIGHT and slowly work their way down the line to see the different displays.

SCADIANS

(ad lib demonstrating crafts to Mother and Child)

After several beats, Mother and Child reach Laurel with Mithril.

LAUREL

(to Mother and Child)

Good morning!

MOTHER

Good morning!

CHILD

Good morning!

MOTHER

(to Laurel)

What is this?

LAUREL

This is my cockatiel Mithril and she is representing parrots in the middle ages. In medieval China cockatoos were important companion animals. They were so popular that by the 12th century they were sacred in Pure Land Buddhism – that's a Chinese form of Buddhism that is a bit different from what they practice in India.

MOTHER

I thought cockatoos were from Australia.

Show Me the Pretty Bird

LAUREL

Not all cockatoos. Many, yes, but several species live throughout the south Pacific, including islands the Chinese explored extensively. But more than that, there is evidence that Chinese explorers did reach northern Australia.

MOTHER

Where are cockatiels from?

LAUREL

New South Wales – which is further south and east than the Chinese reached. But that's okay because Mithril is here as a cockatoo in general. If you look here you see these two plates? The one on the left is food available to parrots in medieval Europe. This is white millet, this is red, almonds of course you recognize, walnuts, and the oats here are from Scotland. Strawberries originally come from Italy. The plate on the right has the millets as well and oranges which we know where domesticated from different citrus plants from south Asia – Vietnam, Thailand, etc. This black looking nut is called kenari and it is an Indonesian almond.

MOTHER

Interesting! How long have you kept birds?

LAUREL

I got my first bird when I was in the third grade. I didn't think about bringing my birds into the SCA until I found out about the other animal sciences that people do. Notably: falconry, house coursing which is a variation on the fox hunt, and there is equestrian where they learn about how to fight on horseback.

MOTHER

How many people study parrots in the middle ages?

LAUREL

There's a lady in Arizona who brings her cockatoo to events and another lady up in Oregon. But I'm the one who does the most research into parrots and how they were kept as pets. This toy here is a cockatiel sized version of a toy we seen in a Jan Steen painting, actually.

MOTHER

Is this your only bird?

LAUREL

Mithril here is a girl. She has a husband named
Aragorn who didn't feel like coming out today. They
have eggs right now and he wanted to sit them.

CHILD

Are your birds going to have babies?

LAUREL

I hope not; my landlord only allows me to have two
birds. Besides, my birds have a lot of eggs. Mithril
wants to be a mommy.

CHILD

That's good!

LAUREL

No, it's bad for her.

CHILD

Why?

LAUREL

Because that's like being pregnant all the time.

CHILD

Why is that bad?

LAUREL

Ask your mother!

Mother and Laurel exchange looks. MOTHER and CHILD
EXIT as LIGHTS FADE OUT.

(END OF SCENE)

<u>Act II, Scene III</u>

2022. April 6. Vine Street Tower apartment, Johnstown, Pennsylvania. WALTER ENTERS from stage left and approaches the bird cage where both Mithril and Arwen are sitting. He proceeds to the water bowls which he empties, washes, and refills before putting them back in their holders. Finding a food bowl filled with Cheerios he goes to a food storage shelf and looks at the selections there.

WALTER

Okay, Laurel said to fill this bowl with cereal. But which one? Cheerios? Lucky Charms? Oatmeal? Hmmm. Well I like the Lucky Charms. Yeah! Lucky Charms! That's what birds want to eat! They are going to love this and Laurel will be so happy when she gets home from the hospital!

Walter dumps the contents of all five food bowls and fills them to the brim with Lucky Charms before putting the bowls back in the cage.

(END OF SCENE)

Act II, Scene IV

2022. April 8. Vine Street Tower apartment, Johnstown, Pennsylvania. LAUREL ENTERS slowly and with clear physical discomfort. Taking off her coat and hanging into the foyer closet, she puts her purse down onto her dining table and crosses over to Mithril and Arwen's cage. Opening the cage she sees it completely devoid of bird food in favor of the Lucky Charms in every bowl.

LAUREL

(frantic)

Oh my God! Walter! What did you do! Birds can't eat Lucky Charms! Why the _____ would you take out all of their food and replace with Lucky Charms? Oh my God! Oh my God!

(Laurel rushes to empty all the food bowls)

Oh Mithril! You poor birdy! Don't worry! I'm here! Let me get you some food!

(Laurel heads to the food canisters containing their seed mixes, Cheerios, and spray millet and refills all the bowls with their proper foods.)

Here you go! Here you go! Come on, babies! Here's some food for you! Oh please! Please be okay! Don't die on me! I need you! I love you! Please don't die!

Mithril chirps reassuredly.

(LIGHTS FADE OUT)

(END OF SCENE)

Act II, Scene V

2023. June. Vine Street Tower apartment, Johnstown, Pennsylvania. LAUREL sits at her desktop computer.

LAUREL

Okay, let's see what is happening on Facebook.

(scrolls down)

Amtrak! They are making improvements to in-seat amenities. Nice! But they still don't allow birds on board. Let's see if I can get them to change that policy. Reply to post: 'when are you going to allow birds on board? I really need to take my cockatiel to the veterinarian in Manhattan. You allow dogs and cats on trains now. Why not pet birds? I have a proper travel cage and am happy to pay to bring them on board.

AMTRAK CONDUCTOR and TOM FACEBOOK ENTER stage right.

AMTRAK CONDUCTOR

Thank you for your query. We presently do not allow birds on our trains. Please see www.amtrak.com for more information.

LAUREL

(replying to Amtrak)

Yes, I know that. But you didn't allow dogs and cats on board before —and now you do. Policies can change. I'm asking you to change your policy and allow birds.

AMTRAK CONDUCTOR

Thank you for your query. We do not allow birds on trains.

TOM FACEBOOK

(replying to Laurel's replies)

Amtrak is NOT a zoo or a pet shop. Leave the animals at home where they belong.

LAUREL

(reading Tom's reply)

Oh my God! What an arse! Right! So I'm never supposed to take my birds to the veterinarian? What a complete jackass! If Amtrak can allow dogs and cats on trains, then they should allow birds. Same for the airlines. When I brought Galadriel and Cleo to New Jersey, all the major airlines allowed birds – some charged more than others and some had shorter windows than others for the vet certificate. But it was possible. Not anymore. United. American Airlines. Both of them have changed their pet policies so that birds are not allowed – not in cabin and not in cargo. Only Delta allows birds on board now.

The question is: do I want to reply to him? Facebook is not exactly a private place to talk to anyone. Hmmm. Hmmm. Maybe I shouldn't reply. I'll just tell my best friend how I feel instead. Peter Capaldi once said that 'being nice is a way of not letting people know you hate them.' I'll be nice in public. But oh my god! What a jackass!

(END OF SCENE)

Act II, Scene VI

2023. Johnstown Pennsylvania. Garden near the Conemaugh River. LAUREL and WALTER ENTER stage left to ducks quacking and song birds singing. Laurel offers some food to the birds before looking across the water.

LAUREL

Beautiful day today.

WALTER

It's okay. At least it's not raining.

LAUREL

The birds are happy. Did you see that beautiful cardinal in the tree as we reached the park? She's getting a nice breakfast.

WALTER

Why do you love birds so much?

LAUREL

I always have. From the moment I saw my first cockatoo at a pet store I knew I wanted them in my life.

WALTER

But it's just a bird!

LAUREL

Just a bird?

WALTER

What is so special about birds?

Show Me the Pretty Bird

LAUREL

(musing and singing "For the Beauty of the Earth")

FOR THE BEAUTY OF THE EARTH. FOR THE BEAUTY OF THE SKIES. FOR THE LOVE WHICH FROM OUR BIRTH OVER AND AROUND US LIES.

LORD OF ALL TO THEE WE RAISE. THIS OUR HYMN OF GRATEFUL PRAISE.

(returning to normal speech)

I love that song. Birds are beautiful! The pinnacle of Creation. There's something holy and precious about birds. Have you ever really, really watched them, Walter? God's majesty revealed in the complexity of their feathers, in the way they communicate with each other. It is truly marvelous!

WALTER

I still don't get why you spend so much time obsessing over them.

LAUREL

I love them. Mithril especially. My dearest and most loyal friend.

WALTER

But she's nearly blind and can't fly.

LAUREL

So? She's beautiful!

WALTER

If you say so.

LAUREL

Don't you think she's pretty?

WALTER

No!

LAUREL

(turning away from Walter and to the audience)

Ad libs astonishment

WALTER

I've never seen the point of animals. I've had dogs.
I've had cats. But they were never allowed to
misbehave.

LAUREL

I, I really have no idea what to say to that. I love
animals. I love birds. People … not so much. Birds
have pure hearts, pure souls. They are beauty,
matchless beauty. Gifts from God.

(END OF SCENE)

Act II, Scene VII

2024. May 6. Vine Street Tower apartment, Johnstown, Pennsylvania. LAUREL sits with Mithril center stage and speaks to her.

LAUREL

You enchant me, bird of my heart.

After twenty years I feel it no less

You beat the odds as a tiny chick

Determined to live when other cockatiels would die.

You've had your share of struggles.

An abusive husband nearly killed you over some eggs.

Colds have nearly taken your life.

Abusive humans have wounded your soul.

Age has taken away your power of flight.

You cannot navigate nor land where you want to.

You cannot see, you cannot reach key feathers when you preen.

Age seems determined to take your life.

Show Me the Pretty Bird

Still you love me.

You fight off every obstacle.

Your will to live inspires everyone.

You refuse to yield to the pain you feel.

White feathers still glow in the shining sun.

I do not know how much time we have left.

How much more can you fight, can you endure?

All I know is you are precious to me.

My life is enriched by your gentle soul.

Even when you bite me and it bleeds.

Stay with me, my Mithril bird.

Stay as long as you can.

For your love is greater than all of humanity
combined.

You are the brightest part of my life.

With you I know I am cherished.

With you I know I am loved.

(END OF SCENE)

(END OF ACT II)

Epilogue

LAUREL stands on the stage apron and addresses the audience one final time.

LAUREL

Well, that's our show! Just a brief introduction to living with birds and all the crazy stuff that really has happened these last few years as a bird lady in a world that is not. Of course there's no way I can communicate what a lifetime of living with birds is all about, but I do hope you have a general feel for it. Thanks for being part of this tale down memory lane. But before we go, let's join our voices altogether to sing Aragorn's favorite song.

(reprising "Sing")

SING, SING A SONG. LET THE WORLD SING ALONG. SING OF LOVE THERE COULD BE. SING FOR YOU AND FOR ME. SING, SING A SONG. MAKE IT SIMPLE TO LAST YOUR WHOLE LIFE LONG. DON'T WORRY THAT IT'S NOT GOOD ENOUGH FOR ANYONE ELSE TO HEAR. JUST SING, SING A SONG!

(to audience)

Come on! Join me!

LA LA LA LA LA LA LA LA LA LA LA LA LA LA
LALA LA LA. LA LA LA LA LA LA LA LA LA LA
LA LA LA LA LA LA LA LA.

(ending)

JUST SING, SING A SONG!

(END OF SCENE)

(THE END)

Production Notes

<u>Songs</u>

<u>Prologue</u>:

The Brady Bunch Theme

Written by Frank De Vol

<u>Act I, Scene VI</u>

It's a Small World

Written by Richard M. Sherman and Robert B. Sherman

Sing

Written by Joe Raposo

<u>Act II, Scene VI</u>

For the Beauty of the Earth

Written by Folliott S. Pierpont

Laurel A. Rockefeller

Epilogue

Sing (reprise)   57

Written by Joe Raposo

Show Me the Pretty Bird

<u>Character Descriptions</u>

Note: Mithril, Arwen, and Aragorn should be cast as stuffed animals or similar toy bird props.

LAUREL

Narrator and author to the play. Bird lady whose love for her cockatiels has no bounds. Wears only dresses and skirts.

MITHRIL

Laurel's whiteface lutino cockatiel hen with all white feathers. Performed by a combination of sound effects and a toy. Mithril's "speech" is a garbled blend of whistles, singing, and normal speech.

ARWEN

Laurel's dominate silver whiteface pied cockatiel hen. Performed by a combination of sound effects and a toy.

ARAGORN

Mithril's husband who is rehomed in 2011 after he tries to kill her. Normal grey male. Loves to sing to his favorite songs. Only says "for really, silly" in regular speech; otherwise all whistles and singing.

KURT

Laurel's roommate in Brooklyn, New York. A drunk with Asperger Syndrome.

SCADIANS

Members of the Society for Creative Anachronism who are hosting a public demonstration of medieval arts and crafts. Dressed in period clothing from across medieval Europe and assorted centuries between 700 CE and 1650 CE. One SCAdian spins with a drop spindle and offers a fiber arts display.

MOTHER

A Brooklynite browsing the demo with her child.

CHILD

A boy or girl roughly six to ten years old.

WALTER

Elderly neighbor in Johnstown Pennsylvania. Knows absolutely nothing about birds. Walks slowly and with the help of a cane.

AMTRAK CONDUCTOR

Amtrak employee.

TOM FACEBOOK

Random Facebook user critical of traveling with birds.

Laurel A. Rockefeller

<u>Characters by Scene</u>

Prologue: Laurel

Act I, Scene I: Laurel

Act I, Scene II: Laurel

Act I, Scene III: Laurel

Act I, Scene IV: Laurel

Act I, Scene V: Laurel

Act I, Scene VI: Laurel

Act II, Scene I: Laurel, Kurt

Act II, Scene II: Laurel, Scadians, Mother, Child

Act II, Scene III: Walter

Act II, Scene IV: Laurel

Act II, Scene V: Laurel, Amtrak Conductor, Tom Facebook

Act II, Scene VI: Laurel, Walter

Act II, Scene VII: Laurel

Epilogue: Laurel

Show Me the Pretty Bird

<u>Settings by Scene</u>

<u>Apartments</u>

Most of this play happens at a very limited number of locations. Those locations are:

- East 19th Street apartment, Brooklyn New York

- Ocean Ave. apartment, Brooklyn New York

- Vine Street Tower apartment, Johnstown, Pennsylvania.

Unless specified otherwise, the bird cage referenced in this play is a large cage sized for a macaw or large cockatoo and approximately the same floor footprint as the modest dining table with its four chairs.

East 19th Street Apartment: A two bedroom apartment. Livingroom features a large computer desk, couch, entertainment center, and coffee table. Above the couch is a large painting with a wide wooden frame.

Ocean Ave. Apartment: a studio apartment. Birdcage is on the opposite side of stage from the kitchen area which includes a stove, sink, refrigerator, and cupboards. Between these are the dining table and bed. The bird cage is approximately the same footprint as the dining table.

Vine Street Tower apartment: a one bedroom apartment. Upstage left is the kitchen with sink, cupboards, and countertops. Upstage right is apartment foyer, entry door, and foyer closet. Bird cage is along center stage left. Downstage left is a computer desk and chair upon which is a desktop computer, mouse, keyboard, etc. Light from a largely unseen window beams onto the computer. A floor length perch stand rests downstage not far from the desk.

Downstage left is a book and DVD filled bookcase. On the top is a cockatiel nest box primarily owned by Arwen.

Show Me the Pretty Bird

Prologue

Bare stage apron

Act I, Scene I

2010. Ocean Ave Apartment

A dining table and chairs. A small bed and related small apartment furniture. Large bird cage is opposite from the kitchen area.

Act I, Scene II

Main stage is curtained off. Stage apron only.

Act I, Scene III

2010. Ocean Ave. apartment

Sink, wall cupboards, and refrigerator. A dining table and chairs. Large bird cage is opposite from the kitchen area.

Act I, Scene IV

2023, July. Vine Street Tower apartment

Desktop computer on desk near window. A chair behind it. Large bird cage is about two feet behind the chair along the same wall.

Act I, Scene V

2024. January 5. Vine Street Tower apartment

Desktop computer on desk near window. A chair behind it. Large bird cage is about two feet behind the chair along the same wall. On the desk top are a computer mouse, mouse pad, and wrist support. Keyboard on shelf beneath. Assorted papers scattered around.

Act I, Scene VI

2010. Ocean Ave. apartment

Large bird cage is opposite from the kitchen area.

Act II, Scene I

East 19th Street Apartment. Livingroom

Computer on computer desk. Office chair. Couch with large painting over it. Coffee table.

Act II, Scene II

Brooklyn, New York. A shelter adjacent to a large field where horses are practicing agility.

A row of tables and chairs. Various medieval crafts on the tables. A drop spindle and wool. A basket of hand spun yarn. At Laurel's station are research papers, small wood/grapevine/leather bird toys, and plates of parrot foods nearby sitting next to Mithril in her travel cage.

Act II, Scene III

Vine Street Tower apartment, Johnstown, Pennsylvania.

Bird cage. Side table with food storage containers filled with various bird foods: seed, Cheerios, millet. Box of Lucky Charms cereal.

Act II, Scene IV

Vine Street Tower apartment, Johnstown, Pennsylvania.

Bird cage. Side table with food storage containers filled with various bird foods: seed, Cheerios, millet

Act II, Scene V

Vine Street Tower apartment, Johnstown, Pennsylvania.

Computer on computer desk.

Act II, Scene VI

2023. Johnstown Pennsylvania. Garden near the Conemaugh River.

A park bench near center stage. Lots of bird noises, including quacks from the ducks in the river and songbirds closer into the park.

Act II, Scene VII

2024. May 6th. Vine Street Tower apartment, Johnstown, Pennsylvania.

A table and chair center stage. Mithril sits on Laurel's lap or on the table.

Epilogue

Bare stage apron

<u>Song Lyrics</u>

<u>It's A Small World</u>

(Richard M. Sherman and Robert B. Sherman, 1963)

It's a world of laughter

A world of tears

It's a world of hopes

And a world of fears

There's so much that we share

That it's time we're aware

It's a small world after all

It's a small world after all

It's a small world after all

It's a small world after all

It's a small, small world

Laurel A. Rockefeller

There is just one moon

And one golden sun

And a smile means

Friendship to ev'ryone

Though the mountains divide

And the oceans are wide

It's a small world after all

It's a small world after all

It's a small world after all

It's a small world after all

It's a small, small world

Show Me the Pretty Bird

<u>Sing</u>

(Joe Raposo, 1971)

Performed by The Carpenters in 1973

Sing, sing a song

Sing out loud

Sing out strong

Sing of good things not bad

Sing of happy not sad

Sing, sing a song

Make it simple to last

Your whole life long

Don't worry that it's not

Good enough for anyone

Else to hear

Just sing, sing a song

Laurel A. Rockefeller

Sing, sing a song

Let the world sing along

Sing of love there could be

Sing for you and for me

Sing, sing a song

Make it simple to last

Your whole life long

Don't worry that it's not

Good enough for anyone

Else to hear

Just sing, sing a song

(Just sing, sing a song)

Just sing, sing a song

Show Me the Pretty Bird

<u>For the Beauty of the Earth</u>

Folliott S. Pierpont, 1864

For the beauty of the earth,

For the beauty of the skies,

For the Love which from our birth

Over and around us lies:

Lord of all to Thee we raise.

This our hymn of grateful praise.